The Fields

The Fields

Poems by

Sean Akerman

© 2025 Sean Akerman. All rights reserved.
This material may not be reproduced in any form, published,
reprinted, recorded, performed, broadcast,
rewritten, or redistributed without
the explicit permission of Sean Akerman.
All such actions are strictly prohibited by law.

Cover design by Shay Culligan
Cover image by Stephen Catterall
Author photo by A. W. Springer

ISBN: 978-1-63980-759-8

Kelsay Books
502 South 1040 East, A-119
American Fork, Utah 84003
Kelsaybooks.com

for Robin,
for Arlo,
for Woody

Contents

Contact	13
Proof	14
Slippage	16
Leonids	18
Third Shift	19
The Order of Things	20
Rear Window	22
Sibling	23
Reading Obituaries	24
Beginner's Mistake	25
Appointment	26
Envy	27
Underground River	28
Field of Vision	29
Weather	31
Epistemophiliac	32
Paranormal Activity	33
Rabbit Rabbit Day	34
Bitterly Cold	35
Dispute	36
Recall	37
Crossing	39
Talking to Myself	40
Taliesin	41
Negative Space	42
Inflation	44
Out of Nothing	45
Middle Years	46
Voyageur	47
Nijinsky Revisited	49
Routine	50
Scrapped Footage	51

Cosmological Principle 53
Outburst 54
Trauma Response 56
History of Reading 58
Conclusion & Dream 59

    Last night you woke me
for a look at Jupiter,

that vast cinder wheeled unblinking
in a bath of galaxies. Watching, we traveled
toward an apprehension all but impossible
to be held onto—

that no point is fixed, that there's no foothold
but roams untethered save by such snells,
such sailor's knots, such stays
and guy wires as are

mainly of our own devising.

        —Amy Clampitt, "A Hermit Thrush"

Contact

Drifting down a ravine thick with cattails
the contact makes true the dream you hailed from & left.
Waver past boughs with snow in your eyes, heat in your ears
toward a silence tender enough to be a cousin.

An atlas was imparted to you prior to memory.
Not imparted, exactly—
there was no giver or occasion, this came before
those norms, the suggestion of a home
vaster than the sea at night,
what you took as a secret.

So many secrets came after. Noise married
the granularity of maps. Truthfully
it has become hard to be alone with yourself.
When you kneel at the base of a certain white pine &
attend to no compass there is a slight hum.

Proof

I must make this up as I go along. No one comes 'round
to hum a dirge & their voices would chafe if they did.

Just imagine: village folk yammering up the hill armed
with their casseroles of tater tots & basic cheese.

Oh, fuck. I can smell it now. Hell is other people,
said Sartre, smoking. Our relations are not corrupted

from the start but can become so, & this,
then, is hell. Once in Lisbon in dry July heat

not far from a black sand beach I listened to fado begin
in a restaurant serving grilled fish & skewered vegetables.

Seafoam paint across the plaza charmed an apartment
where a tsunami rose long ago. Down the forks went

when the first voice swelled. A hush drowned
the tiled walls to show reverence was possible

absent of liturgy. Silence dovetailed over the fleur-de-leis
behind the viola baixo. Hearing this music made me

assume intimacy with a lament of a person no longer here,
as if saudade is a feeling available to rent, authenticity for sale

only elsewhere, the secret of any immigrant's kin,
polite mistrust transmitted in gaze & story deranges

my idea of "the social" & validates solitude's shadow.
It's hard to know where to go from here. After Portugal

I flew to New York & read a novel about the prelude
to the first opium war. At the end, over the sea,

I wept in economy about nothing in my days,
not the impending breakup nor the debt

but how a character bought a painting he couldn't afford
of Canton, to remember such a place existed.

Virgo is ruled by The Hermit, which justifies
my choices. The bearded figure with a lantern

outstretched knows of the mountains behind him,
has been there, or is wise enough not to go.

Little tributes, some turbulence. Perhaps in another life I was
hooded & gathered around stones mumbling to the four winds.

But there is only this life. The one where I glide above
an ocean to arrive at an apartment & not explain myself,

disregard the mail & rush the camera roll to the drug store,
impatient to see vistas overrun by ochre, for proof.

Slippage

The lines are most potent before six a.m. but only when night first unbinds & there is a sense of color. Faint blue of frostbite or melancholy. This is the sort of verbiage I've used to describe landscapes but also drugs & the viewing of a certain type of art. Much of my time has been spent walking under power lines & some moments included witnessing. The ache of train tracks swooping toward their outcomes spliced between cement, electricity. Edison's ghost. Specter of nameless labor. The hope was to draw conclusions about what was unrelated. Trace a purity of seeing to an area beyond the original object. Discerning the levels is a sign of erudition but there is easily slippage. Or at the very least, confusion. In therapy everything must be permitted so long as no one in the room is harmed. Imagine what you will in boundless lust & dismay. I'm trying to figure out when this becomes a problem. Of the suicides I've known most lacked humor. George Carlin explaining the airplane safety lecture when I was a child saved my own life by indirection. It bequeathed no caution when flying but did explicate absurdity in the everyday. In the unlikely event of a sudden change in cabin pressure—translation: roof flies off! Minutiae of language is an antidote to the anchor weight of what we carry but so is the ability to see oneself from afar, to grow bored of one's narrative. The flicker between proximity & distance. Let's be honest though: by the time the boys of my youth hung themselves in the barn they were long past such conversations. It's like trying to stop a relapse when counting out change at the liquor store. From a public health perspective, prevention is key though the funding is lacking. Triage may bring back the dead but it does not answer the question of how to go on. I knew someone who once entered a classroom to present her understanding of a book none of the other students had really read. She sat in the middle of a circle of desks &

acknowledged runs in her stockings. At first she didn't speak of the book. She told a story about growing up in a depressed home outside of Paris, smoking often with her friend while sitting on a bench within a cemetery. Picture Montmartre but subtract the grandeur, she advised. The groundskeeper, a middle aged man with a lisp & a mustache, at one point acknowledged the runs below her knees & offered new stockings if she brought her damaged ones to the cemetery the next day. This went on for months. Why, she asked the class, did the groundskeeper want those stockings? She paused to see who would say it. After silence she offered the correction: he used the stockings to clean the lime from the gravestones, to make the lines of the names more evident in blue morning light.

Leonids

Below Leonids in November the century came to.
Beyond the vanishment of stars, small narcissisms.
These lives orchestrated a valley sorted
by who was lovelorn & without capital.

A mass forgetting that time has been unbearable
for most. Not a mass of silent reverence;
a conspiracy of not seeing.

The train bends along the lake, flanked by timber
to be. At night the route dissolves &
hosts privacies of the forest, then gives way.
The articulated dreams of waking.

Soon there is a festival. A saloon beyond capacity.
More amnesia amid a din, sawdust. Attempts
at divination for a small fee.

Two voices decided this is enough,
the same conclusion spoken in separate tones.
For one, the stars led nowhere, to the realm
of fear or predictability, blurred over a hill.

For the other, the stars were to be followed
through the slivers of storm fronts,
between vultures & drones.

The swell of what felt like a rip tide came
as a memory unowned that must be true.

Third Shift

Cloistered by town-planted maples to the west,
an injured crab apple to the east,
there are two white homes visible from where I live,
both with a three season porch.
In many dreams their likenesses are where I awake
for ablutions, casting aside the army blanket
to search for a guest amid a low hum.
As a people we tend to speak mainly of chronic pain
& acknowledge the behaviors of cats & dogs
but not even that is distinct in these scenes.
If I believe in the prescribed methods
there is an essence to distill from recurrence.
Much like turning left around the continent,
one must invoke not the question of why but how.

Who knows?

The roommates are at large, futons scream flophouse.
There is an aura of space muddled by boxes.
Someone else's silver.
Frost strews under the plastic, a window's skyline,
misting the view: my actual house, kitchen light on,
furnished by uncertain silhouettes.
On the list of impossible acts is seeing oneself
from the outside. Yet somewhere far beyond
the cerebellum sits a thing like a millstone
meting out little efforts, turning wheels all night.

The Order of Things

The orange tabby who materialized from dogwood
with a rabbit in its mouth came before the dream of elevators

opening to some elegant Gotham high-rise peopled
by the peers to whom I feel only indifference, the sort

of emotion toast inspires. Difficulty sequencing. What was real,
or first? Permission was granted not to knock, to hell with piety,

an allowance from the boss, whomever he or she may be,
decision maker cloaked as nightbird without words, convictions

strong nonetheless. I descend to waking life on a federal holiday,
prairie smoke wisping to spring beyond a canvas of dandelions

with some asshole braying on the phone about filets at a casino,
superlatives abound & overuse of the word *filets,* deranging

his vacation. Sounds like flays, the way people become the words
they use, the discontent of civilization correlating with fewer

cellar doors & cedar floors. The cat came back, like a kids' story
minus the rhyming, minus the barbershop pole hat, skin of its prey

flayed on a canine. There is always an incursion on childhood,
it's just the way it is. One day instinct is exposed & the jig is up.

I remember these moments, we all do, when drafts of hell
rose to color outside the pages of *National Geographic.* To be old

is to know these things but now, search beyond violence.
The commons may not register my point. These dreams

are lonesome & so are their directives, walking the days,
having bid that doorman goodnight, an old world courtesy.

Rear Window

Dusk in Sheep Meadow ten years ago watching on screen
Jimmy Stewart one August swamped with the swelter
I felt, as though discomfort stays across decades—
breathy, unflinching, akin to the exhale of a bus—only
this time next to someone else's nostalgia, & how wrought
it was. Her memory not of the film or Grace Kelly but
all the events around its first viewing, consolation or escape,
in some era I could never know of & ask of little.
Other people's histories. The miles radiate, vanish.
Private sufferings cached in the plotline of a thriller to
revisit the way the traumatized repeat exposure
to fragments. *Don't!* Glass breaks! A thunderstorm!
Who isn't always on the verge of knowing? Proving
a murder on the way to romance. Is it enough to build
upon? Black flies arrived as a gestalt. A siren splashed
across tenements, the ones portrayed. The world interferes
on what is remembered in a hush. A scene loses purity
to some minor longing. The reviews agree: a classic.

Sibling

Looking often for the little confirmations of loneliness,
tonight a twin engine plane crosses the edge of Orion's belt.
How easy to picture swaths of those I know & the ones
I must imagine by the pulse of a lampshade,
sorrowed, turning over past tablets in the style of
newspapers stacked in the cellar, the shock
of election outcomes & weather events now dull.
The motion sensor light was triggered by nothing,
a typical reading. No one is me if the mood is just so,
nor a derivative, none tied to a shared loss swaying upstream
as dendrites should. What on this earth is just mine
& how much is felt by & large? Ancient question
posed young to a barren room. Call & response.
Step into the evening alongside dusk, an acre's outline
falling to an anonymous dark, for all intents & purposes
on the way to nothing, memory, imagination, relic.
The sequence. Ask again but phrase it right.
If I can draw close enough to the source
without a witness, does it still count?

Reading Obituaries

A creek thawing in April,
the striations less obvious until blue.
The wind against a loose shutter
in an antecedent of tone.
Imagine death as like something else
finding cause to locate blame or blunder.
The endings of strangers arrive
with some rhyme but often none.
The aorta bursts in the unseen way peonies do,
a yellow hour in June when homeowners shop.
Cells duplicate as hacker code gone haywire,
or as an infantry realizing itself under the stars.
All these approximations.
A departure must groan through the night
across acres to inhabit the land,
Rilke wrote of the old country.

Once, they left a field suspicious
a song played & fled with no music in sight.

Beginner's Mistake

Dogwood flushed red across my field
of vision. Winter strips to an essence.
My tendons smart from the weight I swung,
the ancient movements mimicked wrong.
Regret pools from seventeen years past.
Some minor encounter on a snowless, wind chaffed day
elsewhere, speaking on a philosopher long gone,
the good life he wrote of that I never read.
Caught as a fraud if just briefly, a time
beyond seasons watched bare from afar.
I wonder if this ever stops, the heat of mistake
in red-tinged ears, moving in error to a future
undeserved. In the saga of shame
all background music has ceased,
river flow & birdcall absent.

Appointment

If you can say what your general experiences are
of inflammation we can better gauge at what point
the intolerable becomes the inexplicable yet we enter
into this knowing full well you will grow frustrated
with us, we will chafe you through our questions &
methods until the simple fact of being here becomes
what is wrong—you asking for help, another set of eyes,
the wrong eyes, the encounter gone awry as so many
have before, how in a way we act out the play of history,
not the kind written about but yours, lived, to give you
the distinct & uncanny impression nothing can shift.
That is our gift. Familiarity. But stay. There is so much labor
sussing out the space between intention of the spoken
symptom to its felt mystery it calls to mind the overwhelm
standing in an almost demolished house with the floors gone
between levels, looking less at possibility & more at damage
assessment, so a gesture of mourning, or near mourning.
What shall we call that? The care of late empire, or simply,
nocturne. It grounds us to offer these words, like a greeting
card however unwanted, to confirm you were on our mind,
are on our mind. This isn't about us but in some sense
it must be if the desired response is one of being seen,
the act so hard to ask for, requiring buy-in, a gaze received,
what everyone pictures as poker chips shoved forward
in blind faith or idiocy. Please go on. Tell us
how even the mention of that gesture calls to mind
small violence, how the most mundane sayings are still
indexed for you, kept in your deep catalog of shards &
now see how the heat builds as you cobble it together.

Envy

To awake as an animal without resentment's residue,
the heft of expectation not a bureau shepherded up the stairs.
Reduced to essence: these hours more silent & uncrossed.
Old envy is escape to a mind not wed to the long story,
only the scene. Object permanence. Arrival of guests.
Swaths of days pass with a purity
as they would have if I let them.
In Long Island Sound I swam backwards
to evoke some unfortunate pattern of thought.
Miles away a thunderstorm punctuated night.
Anvil clouds & biblical gestures.
Terror for someone else, background for me,
avoiding splinters on the dock in the shroud
of a towel, cloak of shame denied on the way
to gin. Limes & tonic in all their astringency
activate moments like this, an eternal present.
Imitation of repose: the evening passed.
There was an argument ultimately about the form
the days should take. A construction of words
as graceful as the intention behind the topiaries,
which is to say, not very. Still, entrapping.
Morning had yet to break & sleep was at large.
A brief wish, not for death, for another way.

Underground River

Labyrinth watercourse bending beneath
field & forest—navy striations under clay, under root beds,
keeper of secrets flowing over gypsum, limestone &
where genus of fish uncatalogued move within a system
only known by sonar, dashed reunion to the mapped—
this will not be explained to us.
Nothing revealed. No thank you.
A story untold leagues below the urge
not to cease the words. Feel the weight
of the original question.
This is how it was once?
Confidence pales away, posture slackens
in that time we cannot touch, cannot picture.
Ghosts, but not quite. Not the beloved
decedent at the bedside. A passenger shorter than us,
as they were then, from elsewhere, unbound
to a map or address. There for the flicker
of an instant. How we feel presence,
turn to it, assume majesty, nix it, but hold on.

Field of Vision

Stunned by what the body can do, how soft tissue
can emanate purple as a January dawn smudged by
mill smoke, the intention was always to get a handle

on what was happening, to name a symptom
& reduce to a point. Consider how thwarted love
breaks the lines of poems to transmit a mood to a reader

who won't understand, not the intended reader, at least.
Any act of naming & listening casts into the night,
one's control minor, yet it's there, a choice. An act of seeing

hurls one into an acreage. This can frighten, straining
images in a colander of private despair. Remains gather.
Kiefer's fields lapped in oils & cinders & straw make an echo

one must sit with, failing to avoid a remembrance. Where we
were. The wound is in the collective. The body keeps the score,
it is said. Accounts of near death blend: full spectrum light

& the grace of birds intuited as a vibration & mixed signals
called back & forth across a tunnel. The grid of the mind
blackens, rolling outages in the blazing summer, midnight hours,

humid, when mystery builds. The ecstasies of the saints
were not just grand mals, even if they were also that. It is what
we owe to ourselves not to gloss all experience as wiring.

The enterprise that built the clinics has fared well enough,
the spirit of it all reputable, but we never stopped
being children in the emergency room lobby, blind

to questions of insurance & looking sideways, puzzled,
toward the pedestrian on a gurney. Somehow it became
clear the disasters aren't earned, & yes, that could be you.

Will be, to some measure. Maybe yours won't
transpire in a ravine looking up through the
spangled branches of a cedar, the sun drawing off

to the distant call of an owl. Or maybe it will. Where
does this voice hail from anyway? The one that needs
to speculate, to console, to counter what the eye registers.

Weather

Drafts blow in from the lake in a minor chord
sourced from a place of maritime nightmares, graveyard
of shipwrecks, unmapped latitude where the dead
never rise, cupped in the repose of glacier scrape.
Well, it's Tuesday, someone is in pain.
A once broken wrist spasms to signal a dip
in surface pressure. The sun barely skids.
The wind is blamed for mania. A season ago
I watched cloud walls churn above a Kwik Trip
&, if I can attribute character, pause with lethal poise
before growing diffuse. Everything can kill us
or love us on a whim. Phones blared the order
for a basement retreat then all became
background once more. Now birch is shadowed
against dusk swaying in jest, in doom
on the street corner just north.

Epistemophiliac

November in northern Wisconsin, the day callous
& bright. A murmuration over the bay streaked before
cirrus, the shape of a canvas to project beauty & fear,

take your pick. I read starlings were brought to Gotham
to evoke the work of the Bard then spread four ways
without mercy. All this, today, as I watched tsunamis

in reels from 2011, waves that rival trees steaming
toward Japanese shores with miles of floods
behind. A half hour between thrust fault & land crash

leaves no space to picture the biblical, CGI without
the green screen. Even the glance from pier
to horizon lends no clarity at first. A soundless bugle

until black water folds over sea walls. I should think
one day this all gets better, whatever that means.
Maybe the ardor fades to know. But this is not so.

There is still the wish of tenderness afterwards,
stepping over the damp rubble having seen
some shit, talking until dark of what it was like.

Paranormal Activity

The drawer flung open & silverware flew asunder.
A grainy video, Tuesday in someone else's home.
The still figure, darkened behind the homeowner
doing laundry, is who exactly? One must withhold
judgment re: how others live alongside their dead &
possessed. Events happen just cuz. The unease swells.
What are your intentions? Here the night drains
into a gutter melding symphonically with the bugle
of a mourning dove. Say one thing to disarm
stale moods before tossing the covers:
I am guided by obsessions with regard for little including myself.
Most of what I want is unsaid, ridiculous, & an object of derision.
I measured my acres of shame, & the woods beyond astound me.
It is long past civil twilight, mental status in flux all eve,
dysphoric then elevated. Literalism everywhere,
things taken too seriously. Canvas the rooms,
sleep with the lights on if needed, catalog sicknesses.
Or don't. Nothing can be explained in full.
This house was first drawn. The sodium streetlamps
make one grand, or troubled, in the gaze of a stranger.

Rabbit Rabbit Day

Just as British as ever, shouting a genus up the chimney on the first of the month as the periodicals advised a century ago. The evil is warded off. Or is it? In Devon way back when a white rabbit brought death. More distant relatives stayed mum on lagomorphs while at sea, in search of haddock, eyes squinted toward the gales with dread in their groins. The traces of peasantry are all over, confused & certain. Who touched a doorknob four times before going to the store? At some point decline was more of a practice than an event. Or perhaps their suspicions made it all less worse, harm reduction unseen. Add this to the questions. Each night, genuflect toward photos of those returned to earth or acknowledge the moon as if passing a secret. The compulsions have been diluted, the proof not very strong by now. Astringent taste nonetheless, an effort to hold the world.

Bitterly Cold

The forecast today invokes adverb & adjective to describe
temperatures dangerous to humans & pets alike,
as if when close to the bone there will be brief refuge
in description growing lusher. This will be part of the effort
to fall back towards the shadow of art & literature.
Apologies will be offered, so very belated, with averted eyes,
for having gone absent without leave. There will be a bad sonnet
not spoken aloud & addressed to no one in particular—
an empty room, a book laden with dust, a painting so ignored
it is basically background. The pangs of regret in a day
are hardly catalogued because there are always tasks.
Driving south with velocity so the tires warm & the engine hums
fields undulate with the shimmer of frost refracted under rows
of solar panels. Taupe storage buildings with red rooves interrupt
the landscape to contain someone's multitudes. Inside
boxed artifacts of a divorce for thirty dollars a month
lay a collection of letters once esteemed, promising the moon,
next to the bicycle unused after Armstrong's Grand Tours & lies.
It is painful to remember the time before deceit, but it did exist.
When the furnace is quiet & the night realizes itself,
brief booms can be heard, rafter snappers they called them
back home. A poltergeist. Sap in the nearby maple frozen
to explode. Beams in the wall contracting & expanding.
Contact with a future self. Once, it was all possible.

Dispute

Systolic crests as you mumble threats
like a bitter Sicilian. Rhyme all you want
but your response to complexity may erode you.
Which is not to say that complexity will erode you—
there is a choice, some optimism to be had.
But it has eroded others, or made them
unknowable to themselves, ships in the night.
Each week you hear stories of knives held to throats
& cars driven in madness & the sort of disregard
that drains selfhood of its color & etiquette forsaken.
Anger may be an iceberg. In the frozen depths
live the longings & vulnerabilities too leaden
to surface. But this metaphor is lacking,
plus the author is not even taking ownership
by speaking in the second person.

I remember a wintry night when I sat in car
as I said into a phone what I would not do.
Breath pressed against the windshield
& sleet javelined & nothing mattered
except no. Fairy lights elsewhere blurred
when I shouted to a stunned silence then kept on.
I barely registered my hand as my hand,
my voice as my voice. For a second I saw
the driver, myself, & witnessed a person
embrace danger's arc, hold it in his hand,
study it, & start the engine.

Recall

Pastels & contrails on the solstice. Recall of decade old
directions: go left over pea gravel where the river snakes

on Vermont's border to the memory of labor in a sawmill
turned bar. I've earned this relief, or someone has.

Scenes without feeling or purpose stick around.
The plot to a mediocre film on police corruption stays

from one dreary winter night even longer ago, neither art
nor entertainment but time filling, watching water pour.

In the minor longings of a children's book is a summer wish
to live forever & remain astounded. Hoard the days.

When did this change? Driving south out of town
past the remnants of a game farm I am assailed

by a report on flooding thirty years ago, half a continent
away, a culvert teeming after rain & derecho, what was

no great tragedy or wound. My life may be less what I intend
& more the overlay on what occurs. There are some choices.

Lupines bookend a two-lane for an entire half mile
& in the distance KOA has manicured the evergreens.

There is no pressure to visit the historical society. There,
a taxidermized snowy owl perches above swamper axes

rusting beyond use. I attend to what I want & hold
the rest at bay, blurred & muted. The daylight unfurls

between notes of sweetgrass, errands nearby, to be
referenced & kept for a later time, this private index.

Crossing

An evening drive home through December rain, topography comes into focus through thinly grassed wetland, drawn by a headlight's shimmer. Flat pools of ink blue reduce a map like a child painting a landscape. Crossing Brooklyn Ferry, Whitman observed the dark throwing its patches upon him. You look outward to clarify this. As far as you can imagine the river becomes guesswork all the way back to its spring-fed birth. Interference upstream where pig shit & fertilizer move with the weight of destiny from crowded troughs styled on the masses; runoff slides down hills once parted by glaciers, like a ghost at first, through fragrant dawns & starlit evenings lake bound to demand oxygen, still cloaked, where a chorus is joined: nanomaterials, perflourinated compounds, pharmaceuticals. The unseen no longer can be pronounced. You cannot know what glimmered before your birth, care little for the debates after your death. Invisibly at first & then inferred by what long gone artists have urged, the task is to understand where you are with what should not be here. You are not alone, but how exactly? This is the way poems grow up past midnight & circle the great wound.

Talking to Myself

At some point I realized most of what I wanted
to say would never be audible like radio static growing
louder, almost lucid before vanishing as the car speeds

out of town. "Sympathy for the Devil" comes on to calm
the passenger, fill the unease. Speech therapy is central
to democracy even if kids are largely eating cookies

while missing a spelling test. If anything I learned
the stutter had ancient power to demonstrate formation
painstaking as it may be. This, of course, was not emphasized

but implied. The question of audience can't be ignored.
In streets alone & wandering vacant homes I have said words
vile & certain, but who hasn't? I coach people to speak

to an empty chair now. It fails as it is not novel. This is how
our privacies go: stuck in a labor of rehearsal for a play
never staged. Look, the understudies are staring at the rafters.

Taliesin

Floods draped the roads to the estate Frank Lloyd Wright built to return, ultimately, to earth, to shamble in relative silence on the way to regolith. A studio evoked the plains, the hill it grew from, the driftless limestone. With congruence between inner & outer real questions can emerge. Questions without warning after the silence of years, posed to no one & divorced from anxiety's panting, have always been there, as totems, voiced from the encircling dead into a fine ether, found again. At the hearthstone emanated no flame, not the semblance of one, but my memory of a dinner guest some liquid evening ago who told a story of a simple dish crowned with basil, this meal he made for the living that clarified some saga, the details now gone or not faint enough for imprint but a feeling stayed, the answer to a question almost heard.

Negative Space

His time is sketched by what he didn't quite see,
what he glimpsed through a corner of the rearview,
shaded fingers of clouds touching earth

before the car sped over the hill. Once, clotted in traffic
on the plains when a sky turned emerald in the zagged rain,
an expectation was unmet, waiting, scanning for it—

then nothing. Even if he stays, the wonder never arrives.
This came to be the lesson: he can never get any closer
than watching Helen Hunt & Bill Paxton chase twisters

& reckon with their feelings. Circumstance withholds
the way a dream frustrates its plot in the morning.
A relative told him she came to the States fervent

avenues were paved in gold, the residue of a film.
Even after half a century of gravel, concrete dusted
with the rime of pigeon shit, potholes, she still asked:

is there a gilded street in a place I haven't been?
Belief doesn't end & it may not even fade.
The problem with being moved by art is the desire

to be everywhere. Recall how the lights circled
as starlings do, frantic toward a brief form.
Several the color of rust. If he trusted anyone,

it was because they ventured, or were willing to,
the nemesis of an accountant. December, the solstice
close, he walked in the near dark beside a dog

below the faint outline of a craft, not quite a cargo plane,
scooting across the sky, slow. See him then setting a style:
to stumble in the faded day not alone confirming the possible

world. It paused in the sky, as a bird cannot. He drives now
past cornfields lathed in hoarfrost attentive to what may
be disclosed, a return, really, from the quest of yesteryear—

those evenings when he was so drunk, an era of nights,
never mornings, self-portrait at one time, waiting always
in the lobby between hope & dread for the unsaid

to avail itself. The anxiety was arrhythmic, sweat
in the clavicle, four in the morning. The shame hung,
vexed as burlap. Some problems are not so much solved

as outgrown, said a therapist. Does any poet have
an actual range or are they simply flailing in the dark
to find the same feeling from new angles again & again,

a kept man or woman to the centripetal pull of absence?
Circles grow larger but stay circles. It's fair to want more.
It's okay to be unglad & wish beyond literalism, the way

the non-secular among us ask the same questions on the faith
of new angels again & again, how millions wake to pause
for the visitation of a mourning dove, an incarnation of whom?

Inflation

Local dipshit running his mouth again
loathes poetry but will get a poem anyhow.

Cowabunga. His white truck sails the horizon.
Diesel chariot bugles a song of Jack & Diane

to herald homemade sausage, to confirm
what billboards say: real men love babies

or even if not the world as is must be validated
still. This was the great lesson of his schooling

despite detention halls in a luddite time,
all those hours to think & stew & dread

what he could not foresee, what encircles him
now against which he rages. Bait, beer, & ice cream

are expensive. Fucking inflation. In his time,
children wielded chainsaws. Today curricula

for his brethren & the nation at large lack
heart attack courage. Where did it go?

In what hereafter is this? He awakes & won't
ask, shudders, smoking from his porch steps.

Out of Nothing

Chalky light floods from a neighbor's upstairs room.
It's two a.m. & you're awake for a spell, roused
by no rhythm you can name.

The first time you drove alone after dark
you saw a tennis net splayed across the interstate,
or you thought you did.
A checker formation strung long across route 202.
Streetlamp & moonless evening mixed gully & fern.
The feeling stayed until you crossed the mirage,
your heart rate high all the while, & after.
Most of what matters is elsewhere
or dreamt up. A part of you trusted continuation:
space & time as known—Tuesday thinking.
And a part of you stayed unbound.

The faith you need hails from a field beyond memory.
If you had your way you would canvass the hills
for space crafts & never do paperwork.
Speak to ghosts as you take out your dogs at night.
Make exquisite lunches for the commons.

Middle Years

Aloe thrives from neglect. Schefflera evokes hardiness
despite a drafty window & apologetic watering,
the inattention of a not good enough parent.
This is what you're compelled to judge daily
but often don't. The longer you spend in human services
the less certain you are. How to assign blame.
Said an analyst once: within three generations an alcoholic
family will destroy itself if no one tends to the troubles.
Obliteration without comment. Smoke folding in
droves across a plain. No one is doing well.
In rooms of curated lighting & budget couches
months pass. You awake in the dark to write poems
before oatmeal, throw weights around your basement
with "Mr. Brightside" in your ears. It's safe to say
no one called this. You trace lines but they turn
askew. The miles keep coming.

Voyageur

Airborne tracking the stem of the Mississippi
north, a dreamy funk. O to witness early geology.
The wish of impossible privacy to spy Laurentia dividing,
old moment of epic drift. Or a different sort of breech:
to call out to Berryman before he leapt. *Hey hold on a second,
I have a question.* But there are only tributaries to follow into
subdivisions where cups runneth over with the flourish
of clickbait & desire too plain. Cultural criticism is a
new pastime. Please, no more longing, says a whisper
invented. Sawmills are now taprooms evoking a palette
& where fur traders once paddled hard trading posts
have been remade to house meditations urging
presence, messengers in lycra, tones of maxims
not believed in full, yet nearly, carrying in a
wavered voice the loss of any translation.
Was the conversion real or hoped for?
What would it mean to be here now?
What avenues open in your heart
accepting this is the last place
you'll ever know?

You have traveled far. You come to acknowledge
the riverine themes & where you fit, aftermaths
of another age along clay banks snaking against
boreal shores, the seiche out, all sistered between
the screech of tourism & ore docks shuttered,
cul-de-sacs backgrounding amber clouds,
the metallic wash of synthetic drugs.

When history stopped availing itself with fervor
& your heart rose from its concave place
there was a choice. It was posed by no one
& not even spoken to an interiority but became
obvious, the silent lettering of a walk when
the mood shifts, the mood of a personal epoch.

Now it is winter, a Dalmatian pattern of snow
drapes over twin wetlands, burnished gold
below softly purpled skies.
Road work untended, an opinion forms on taxes.
You read in the long defoliated hardwoods a plague
of gypsy moths. How this story will play is almost utterly
out of your hands, the hours of planning & avoidance
misspent. If there is a time to attend it has come,
to fold yourself into the instants
that never asked for commentary anyway.
You walk on a ground laden with the needles
of red pines, swallowed from afar
by the long silhouettes,
another voyageur bound.

Nijinsky Revisited

Neither a sigh nor a postcard would do this time. Since I first wrote to you I discovered that not only were you Polish but the flux of your abdominal muscles, which turned in *Petrouchka,* withstood the highest brimstone of lactic acid. In the last winter you drove a sled recklessly & became vulgar on the issue of vegetarianism. A cross the mass of a stake rested on your chest as you scoured the village. Your wife observed, weeping in her Victorian room. I write to you nostalgic over some lost purity I never knew. No videos exist of you as a puppet on stage, so I guess. Once on the shore at Brighton Beach, I saw the stern practice of glissade among dancers far from their home. I wonder if they look like the ones you knew, who crouched low beside you in a warehouse. Does the waning sunlight harden their faces once they are dressed in black? These questions should seem less onerous than the ones raised by your followers, obsessed with decline. They all searched for a reason when you left. Your feet were cut open to see if perhaps you were half-bird, or if there were springs instead of calcium in your bones. But your insides were just like the man I saw today in a black tunic who wore it as though it was cast on him by another century. Your own black tunic, the play with nymphs, your general androgyny in all my matted photos, topples the greatest myth. I read your universal system of dance & tried a few steps, but my ligaments constrict. Someone misunderstood wrote a system of music that was laughed away from Paris. Entangle them & there is no limit to grace. We haven't caught up to your grammar yet & it's possible we never will.

Routine

To activate, behaviorally speaking, I shower & floss.
Above my right incisor, bone can be seen.
Internally, vitamins gather with minerals to aid
currents that predate all my commentary.
Mirrors are studied for answers like the James Webb telescope,
fewer pastels & less awe, however. Under the same bulb
vigor can rush in the fashion of a log flume hours before
feeling as if in very late style, beyond desire,
only settling the question of integrity versus despair.
This body, this one time deal, awaits congratulations
in a land ruled by diabetes & hypertension.
If nature & nurture were overcome, I never heard.
The lift strains at times, comrades, I do confess.
In the evening I split aspen & praise
my form. Ligaments intact, a certain grace is achieved.
But this has to stop. Not the ardor, just the counting,
the open palm for glory.

Scrapped Footage

Lots of questions around cause &
effect, or, more specifically, asking

how did loss create the wish for union, a pursuit
of ideals across institutions, states, & borders?

A dissertation would be too complex.
Ultimately, it would ask more than it could

answer. There are always the movies but
my time is not that interesting if condensed

to a feature film. Panned by critics, a few parts
would be regarded by nerds for what was

evoked: the persistence of fantasy to sustain
a self. Look at how reverie gathered in a hush

from the passenger side to allude to grandeur
& the exotic throughout regions. The daydreams.

I never did return home from the Himalayas
laden with dirt & a pendant unmentioned

but it was pleasant to conjure even if it painted
over a minute or an hour. Was someone talking?

Most of what I pictured I can't even recall now.
The dead walked down a shaded hill,

clad in flannel yet the words mumbled.
That one stayed, unfinished as it was.

And so have the acts of heroism, flogging
the sons of autocrats or reviving a patient.

I don't ask for help, a sign of the
obvious. Of course I have problems.

The lamp flickers still & the reels pile at my feet,
some upside down while the door's lock sticks a little.

Cosmological Principle

The shadow of discontent has planed across your face.
Not only has there been no resolution to the wounds,
the same dangers resurface in the lake of your time,
indistinguishable from the ones before—
low New England shrubbery hugging a boreal shoreline
with a flotilla of rocks jagged in the shallows,
nameless cabins in the distance where you tried to feel
the embrace of the collective, where you interpreted
what the light implied to allow congruence.
See your brothers & sisters move behind
double-paned windows in quiet efforts to recall
what was almost there. See them stand with uneven pride
having cured themselves of a malady never named.
Depression is the wrong word. How can illness be a cure?
A sigh meets a lack of novelty, when there is less pining
between the blinks of radio towers, more acknowledgment
of a transmission lost once again. Don't fret. This is the law
writ small, what you were born into: the uniform structures
in any life, local variations, sure. Remember the way
a supernova looks the same from all locations,
in a universe without an edge, this possible solace
to your displeasure: to be inside,
finally, the intention not your own.

Outburst

Then, a silence like a surrender.
What you later said was not the wound,
the wound cannot be described, it can only
be circled, guessed at, the way a town plots

its commerce portside, extraction
point unknown. Language at large,
faint translation of intention to deaf ears
following grade school dictums,

just as lost then as now, bridging eras,
a part of the problem, really. After all,
feelings aren't shared, & you aren't even sure
where they end. Pain has taken you away

from the heart of the matter, prescriptions
have dulled the referent. The pulse, your pulse,
thumps through stimulants, forward instead of
searching. Depth foresworn. Is that the trouble?

Talk about the body so as not to talk
of its interiors; or, speak of its interiors
as if they are literal, as if they never stood by
the virtues. And now, Jesus Christ, the wind bays!

Blame sunrise, or the wolves if you want
to distract that way, or the government.
Monastic life appeals. But do they allow
the long recall of fantasies over soup?

Is silence expected in the refectory? Something
has to change & I sense you're close to a choice.
Without urging decline comes. Yesterday you drew
The Moon, not a picture of the hangnail in the night

sky, but what fell from a deck of tarot.
There was a crayfish leaving the sea.
A mountain path. You seem a bit different today.
The tv is off in your room & the window is open.

Trauma Response

On your walk to get smokes you rehearse
how to cope in the event of mass infection,

when calamity roars. Get ready, for there is always
a barn, crimson & vacant, with tall grass

drifting against its boards, the background where
the dead walk their side march as though

they swallowed all the benzos. In another scenario
someone pours asbestos into your blood,

not quite a mad scientist ordeal, more
an argument gone awry, hellscape

in a manufacturing plant. When dusk comes
discernment is impossible, the true horror,

while questions flow as if through a spigot,
the metaphor once used to name anxiety's arc.

Is the light still streaming in through
the torn atmosphere? Is the sound of bells

only a recording? What is that gesture
before disagreement? Remember how something

was afoot in the museum, how chilled you were
at the empty plazas of a de Chirico painting?

Remember the stillness of a couch at eight p.m.
in an unpeopled room filmed by David Lynch?

It is as though you look always for a guest
of great magnitude only to stay caught

choosing who you'd be: the derelict drifter
who says *whatever* as you plunder or

the stunned widower cobbling together a life
you thought you had, speaking to the empty chair

at the dinner table. Bet the farm it'll happen,
not what you picture nor the zombies,

necessarily, but an event on the edges
of dread. Vigilance has taken you this far.

A go bag hangs by the door, the limited imagination.
The rest of the way asks for adaptive tactics, new moods.

History of Reading

The early hope of literacy was to know the emissaries
of elsewhere & sidle into their codes, a fool's errand,
moved I was by lush phrases. And such swaddled comfort
with ghosts, becoming a person who explains myself
through books, where the dead changed not just status
but methods of communication. Yes, there was always a plot
for the professors to unravel & no, that was not the point,
to clarify it, Sherlock Holmes style, as a young Basil Rathbone
would stoic over the moor. It's untellable to know how
it will play from the point of creation, any art, that is,
the urge swaying in the lunar dark ages later,
like an elderly star emitting dust after dormancy,
old smokers, they're called. Walk past the sitting rooms
of neighbors to note the vortex of television in a swirl of another
sort of smoke, asking everything of attention, winking & nodding
like a huckster under the carnival tent. Vigilant at the window
my dog growls when I turn the channels, for an instant only
as mouthy characters refract off the glass & impose
a brief scene on the rain garden he otherwise knows,
an overlay of lawyers & detectives across milkweed & aster.
Eventually I wanted fewer reference points, a cleaner lens
to glimpse the uncut field of these days in the spirit of how
he perhaps prefers the silence, the watching, waiting
for the real.

Conclusion & Dream

In the home of your youth the siding stays cedar,
the smell of cheese redolent still, from a factory
that caked the foundation long vanished, even more
vanished thirty years after its slight remembrance,
the way childhood observes almost nothing & absorbs
almost everything. Your dream was a work of architecture.
A wrestling ring where you channeled your lust & fury
was remade to fence in your dogs. A hemlock where you spied
disorderly conduct grew yellow & metallic, rising high
toward the sun. A dream grants some wishes yet must
build you elsewhere. So it is you enter the kitchen:
the linoleum darkens, & near a bay window hums a pellet stove,
suggesting presence when there is none. Your name is scrawled
upstairs, misspelled, on the plastered wall of a crawl space.
Hard to tell what is artifact, what is prophecy as you reckon
with origins to follow a long tunnel over stones shadowed
under the flickers of torchlight, into what appears to be a tomb,
or a scene of a tomb from a movie you half-remember. You turn
away from where it leads, from any conclusion, even this,
the gesture that has lasted over the roads & fields & years.
The woodpile bends against the shed, the grass
is uncut, tinged ivory, & swept west by the wind.

About the Author

Sean Akerman is a poet, novelist, and writer of nonfiction. Born and raised in the lakes region of Maine, he later moved to New York City, where he earned a PhD in psychology from the City University of New York. He went on to hold faculty appointments at Hunter College, Sarah Lawrence College, and Bennington College. Now he works as a therapist amid the varieties of trauma.

His books include: the novel, *Outposts* (Threekookaburras, 2017); the novella, *Krakow* (Harvard Square Editions, 2018); the poetry collections, *The Magnitudes* (Main Street Rag Publications, 2019) and *Bridges, Night* (Kelsay Books, 2023); as well as a study of exile, *Words & Wounds* (Oxford University Press, 2019). He resides in the North Woods near Lake Superior's south shore.

www.ingramcontent.com/pod-product-compliance
Lightning Source LLC
Chambersburg PA
CBHW071013160426
43193CB00012B/2035